GW00418927

# JAZZ PIANO AURAL TESTS
## GRADES 4 & 5

# ABRSM

© 1998 by The Associated Board of the Royal Schools of Music
Published by ABRSM (Publishing) Ltd, a wholly owned subsidiary of ABRSM
Printed in England by Caligraving Ltd, Thetford, Norfolk, on materials from sustainable sources
Reprinted in 2017

# Introduction

Aural and musicianship skills are a fundamental part of jazz performance and improvisation. In solo work jazz musicians must hear in their head the rhythmic and harmonic context in which they are working, in order to respond inventively and stylistically to that sound in their improvisation. In ensemble playing musicians must make choices about their role within the overall texture and the notes or rhythms that are most appropriate to play in the light of what they hear. ABRSM's aural tests are designed to help you to listen to music in this way and to foster working by ear, the best and often the only way to learn jazz.

## The Practice Tests

The practice tests, provided here as an accompaniment to the ABRSM syllabus, can also be extended into fun exercises for developing improvisation and other jazz skills. Preparation for the tests involves doing the same activities as learning new pieces or practising the improvised sections, and you should therefore see them as a natural and familiar part of your learning experience. Questions along the lines of 'What feel is this in?', 'How many beats in a bar are there?', 'How does this rhythm go?', 'What's the tune?' and 'Can you clap the pulse?' are almost bound to occur in the course of learning pieces and developing improvisation skills. It is these sorts of questions that the examiner asks in the aural tests.

The chapter on the aural tests in *Jazz Piano from Scratch* suggests several activities for the development of these vital skills. *Jazz Piano: The CD* (available for each grade separately), which illustrates how each element of the aural tests will be presented in the exam and also records several of the A Tests, is a further invaluable resource for the extension of your work. Each recorded test is indicated by the symbol (CD) in this book.

## Test A

This test consists of several elements, based on a single piece of music heard, as follows:

*A1: Stating the time and groove*
A1 practises your ability to count along with a given short piece — if you like, to play along in your head — and to have the confidence to state its time. Remember that while the first beat may be stressed, swing and rock grooves have regular and irregular stresses on other beats too, often two and four, so looking for regular sequences of stresses will help. You must also identify the groove (swing, rock or latin) of the piece.

*A2: Clapping on a specified beat or sub-beat of the bar*
This second part of the test is designed to develop the important jazz skill of rhythmic flexibility, whereby a player is able to place a note or chord, or begin a musical phrase, at any point desired in the bar. The examiner will tell you on which beat or sub-beat you should clap and will then state the time, count in and play the piece again. You must join in from the first bar with an accurate, confident and relaxed articulation of the beat specified. Remember that if you are asked to clap on the sub-beat, the feel, either swing or straight, must be reflected.

*A3: Clapping the rhythm of a short extract*

Hearing a rhythm and copying it exactly, including articulation and phrasing where appropriate, is the skill here. The examiner will play twice a short extract from the music played for A1 and A2, and you should clap it back. Concentrate on keeping a steady pulse as well as accurately reproducing the extract. Remember to keep going, even if you make a mistake.

## Test B

*B1: Question and answer/improvised answering phrases*

Question and answer is an invaluable technique used by improvisers and composers in jazz all the time; they will invent melodies which contain answering phrases, or play 'fours', where one musician plays a question and another responds to it.

Test B1 requires you to respond to four two-bar phrases, played by the examiner, with an improvised answering phrase. You should be able to reproduce something of the style of the given phrase within a simple yet effective improvisation, and this may be done with the voice or at the piano. The examiner will be looking for a flexible and creative response to the question, as well as evidence that you have identified the given rhythmic style and tempo and can work within it. Your improvised answers may use such musical devices as the reproduction of elements of the question (without copying it entirely!) and the use of common jazz devices for creating rhythmic interest, including dynamics, leaving gaps, use of surprise, polyrhythm, and varying stressed and unstressed notes.

This book contains several B tests for you to work on. Remember that, as with Test A, these practice tests are simply the starting-points for extended work on your aural skills. Once your teacher or friend has played the notated phrases and you have responded to them, get him or her to play the given groove round and round, inventing different questions for you to respond to, and really 'get into the groove'. The last page of the Test B section for each grade contains some extra grooves for you to work on with this activity in mind.

You will notice that the syllabus states you can either sing or play your answering response. If you play, bear in mind that the examiner will also be at the piano, so you will sit to the right of the examiner and your response will have to be played up an octave.

*B2: Singing and identifying intervals*

The examiner will ask you to sing and identify two melodic intervals. *Jazz Piano from Scratch* gives some useful hints on how to prepare for this part of the exam. Remember that the examiner is looking for accurate and confident pitching, not for a beautiful vocal tone.

## Summary

Jazz musicians use their aural and analytical skills to fix a clear and detailed inner aural image, or 'internal map', of a piece of music in their heads. This map will provide the structure — important rhythmic, melodic, harmonic and formal features — upon which any successful improvisation will be made. Developing and working on your aural skills is not something that will stop at Grade 5; it is something you will continue to do for the rest of your life as a jazz musician. It is, however, a fundamental and hugely satisfying part of jazz.

*Charles Beale*

# GRADE 4

## Test A

**A1** To state the time of a passage of music in 2, 3 or 4 time played by the examiner and to identify the groove as swing, rock or latin.

**A2** To clap on the fourth or last quaver of each bar, chosen by the examiner, while the above passage is played again. The examiner will first state the time and count in the candidate.

**A3** To clap the rhythm of a short, single-line extract (marked 'X') from the above passage played twice by the examiner.

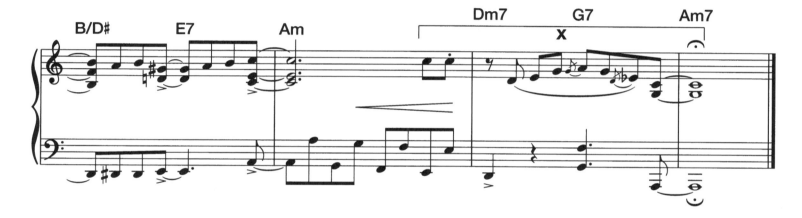

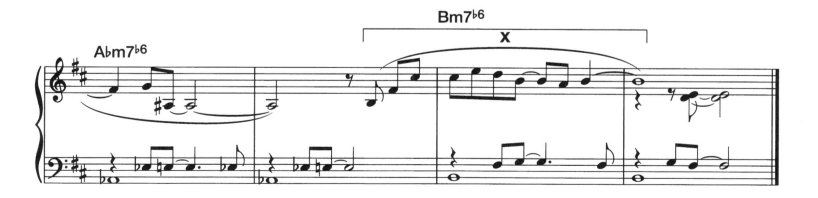

# GRADE 4　　Test A

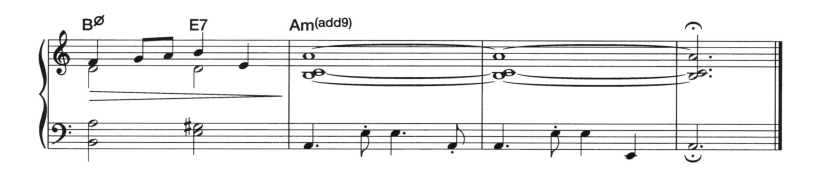

**Straight 8s Calypso**　♩ = 72

# GRADE 4    Test A

# GRADE 4    Test A

## GRADE 4　　Test A

**Straight 8s Rock**　♩ = 104　**Train Boogie**

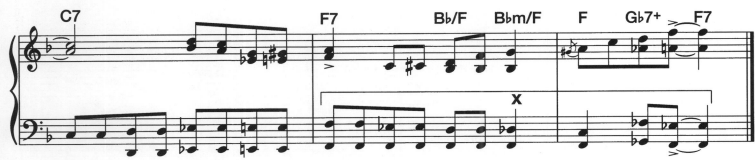

**Straight 8s Latin**　♩ = 126

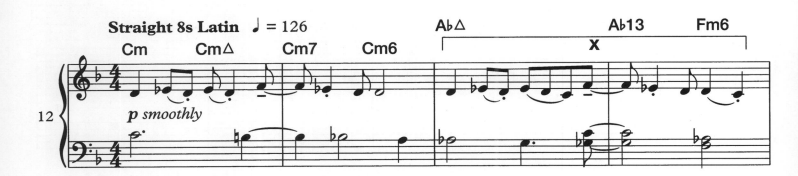

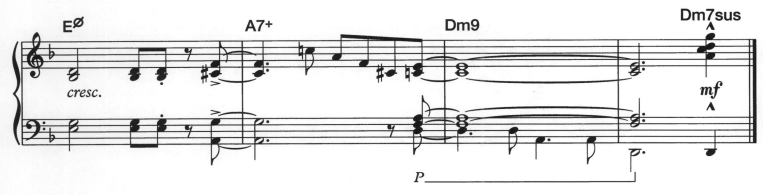

# GRADE 4  Test A

# GRADE 4

## Test B

**B1** To sing or play improvised answering phrases to four two-bar phrases in a major or minor key or mode played by the examiner. The answers should follow each phrase in strict time without an intervening pause. The key-chord or chord on the root will first be named and sounded, and the pulse given. The examiner will then play four bars introductory groove, before playing the first phrase to which the candidate should respond, and continue with an accompanying groove throughout the test.

**B2** To sing and identify two melodic intervals limited to a major second, major and minor third, perfect fourth and perfect fifth, as used in the above four short phrases, after the examiner has played them twice.

GRADE 4    Test B

# GRADE 4   Test B

# GRADE 4    Test B

# GRADE 4    Test B

These extra grooves provide further practice for Test B. Get your teacher or friend to invent two-bar right-hand questions over them and improvise your own two-bar answers.

# GRADE 5

## Test A

**A1**   To state the time of a passage of music in 2, 3, 4 or 5 time played by the examiner and to identify the groove as swing, rock or latin.

**A2**   To clap on a set quaver of each bar, chosen by the examiner, while the above passage is played again. The examiner will first state the time and count in the candidate.

**A3**   To clap the rhythm of a short, single-line extract (marked 'X') from the above passage played twice by the examiner.

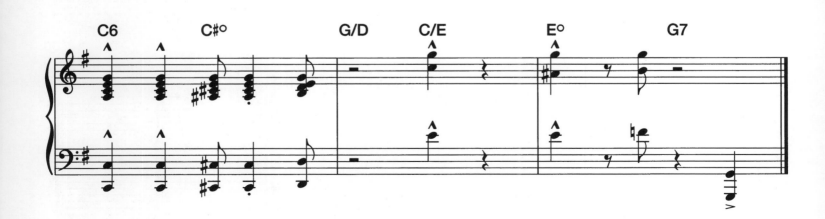

# GRADE 5    Test A

# GRADE 5 Test A

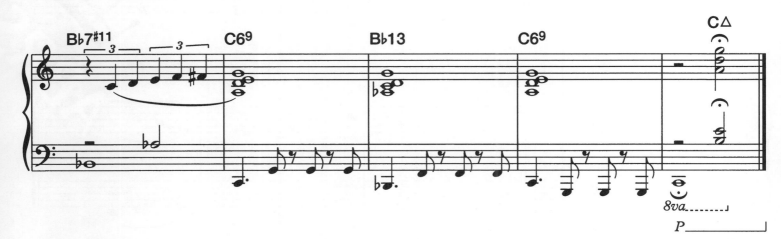

# GRADE 5    Test A

# GRADE 5    Test A

# GRADE 5 Test A

# GRADE 5   Test A

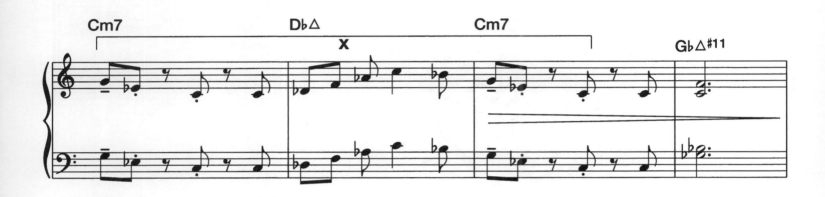

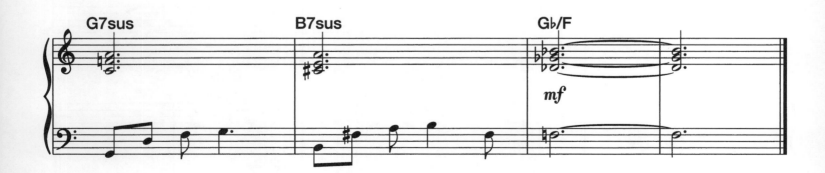

GRADE 5    Test A

# GRADE 5

## Test B

**B1** To sing or play improvised answering phrases to four two-bar phrases in a major or minor key or mode played by the examiner. The answers should follow each phrase in strict time without an intervening pause. The key-chord or chord on the root will first be named and sounded, and the pulse given. The examiner will then play four bars introductory groove, before playing the first phrase to which the candidate should respond, and continue with an accompanying groove throughout the test.

**B2** To sing and identify two melodic intervals limited to a major and minor second, major and minor third, perfect fourth, perfect fifth, and major and minor sixth, as used in the above four short phrases, after the examiner has played them twice.

## GRADE 5    Test B

*\* omit grace-note for interval test*    AB 2679

# GRADE 5    Test B

# GRADE 5    Test B

**Swing** ♩ = 144 **Quasi 'The Waltz you Swang'**

# GRADE 5    Test B

# GRADE 5    Test B

These extra grooves provide further practice for Test B. Get your teacher or friend to invent two-bar right-hand questions over them and improvise your own two-bar answers.

**Straight 8s Latin**  ♩ = 112

**Straight 8s Rock**  ♩ = 100

**Swing**  ♩ = 144

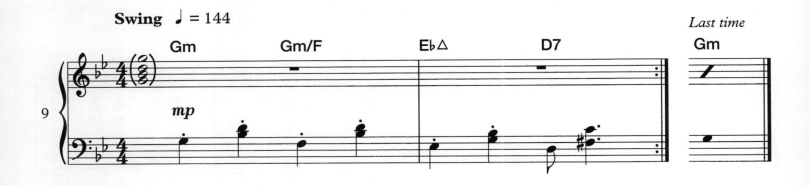

**Straight 8s Latin (Rumba)**  ♩ = 138

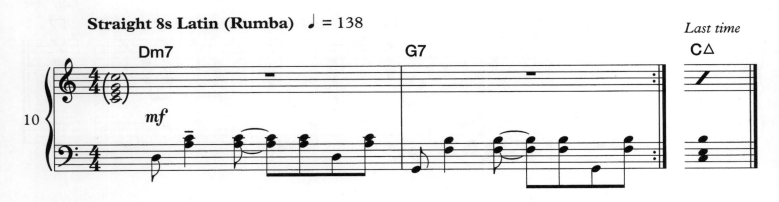